EDWARDIAN ANGLESEY

A Pictorial History

Volume 2

by

John Cowell

© Copyright John Cowell, 1992

All rights reserved. No part of this publication may be reproduced or transmitted in any form or by any means, electronically or mechanically, including photocopying, recording or any information storage or retrieval system, without prior permission in writing from the author.

First published in 1992

ISBN: 0 9518592 1 8

Typeset and printed in Wales by W.O. Jones (Printers) Ltd., Llangefni, Anglesey, Gwynedd LL77 7EH

LIST OF ILLUSTRATIONS

Aberffraw, 107
Amlwch, 76-87
Beaumaris, 26-37
Benllech, 48-49
Bodedern, 105
Bodffordd, 69
Bodorgan, 108-109
Bull Bay, 88
Caergeiliog, 114
Cemaes, 89-93
Gaerwen, 117-119
Glyn Garth, 23

Gwalchmai, 115-116
Holland Arms, 120
Holyhead, 94-101
Llanddwyn, 111
Llandegfan, 22
LLanerchymedd, 71-73
Llanfaes, 38-39
Llanfairpwll, 122-128, 131
Llangefni, 50-68
Llangoed, 40-41
Llangwyllog, 70
Malltraeth, 110

Menai Bridge, 4-21
Nebo, 75
Newborough, 112-113
Penmon, 42-44
Penmynydd, 45
Pentraeth, 46-47
Plas Newydd, 129-130
Rhosgoch, 74
Rhosneigr, 106
Tal-y-Foel, 121
Trearddur Bay, 102-103
Valley, 104

The cover illustration shows a peaceful scene on Menai Bridge promenade during the summer of 1905. This was a popular place to take a quiet stroll and to enjoy the sea air on the adjoining pier.

PREFACE

This book is intended to complement the first volume of *Edwardian Anglesey* and therefore has much the same format. The illustrations have been selected for their photographic quality and for their importance as documents of social history, and in many ways they are more vivid than the written word. Facts have been derived, wherever possible, from contemporary sources. These include local newspapers and periodicals, business directories, council minute books, Parliamentary Papers, Census Returns and various manuscript collections at the County Record Office, Llangefni, the University College, Bangor, and the Post Office Archives, London. A list of published sources of local interest appeared at the end of Volume 1.

I acknowledge with profound gratitude the courteous assistance received from Mr Einion Thomas, the Archivist at the County Record Office, Llangefni, and Mr Tomos Roberts, the Archivist at the University College of North Wales, each of whom gave me a great deal of help. I am also deeply indebted to Mr Handel Evans for granting me access to the rich collection of slides housed at the County Library, Llangefni, and for permission to have some of them copied. My thanks are also due to Mr Jeff Morris for allowing me to quote from his book *The Closed Lifeboat Stations of Anglesey*, and to the countless other kind people who so willingly supplied information not found elsewhere. Any errors of fact are entirely my own.

I am especially grateful to the following for their generosity in allowing me to reproduce original photographs as illustrations in the book: Mrs Gwen Brindle Owen, *pages* 28, 55, 56, 57, 59, 60, 61, 69, 105, 108, 110, 112; Mr. William Evans, 50, 51, 52, 54, 58, 62, 64, 73, 109, 118; Mrs Bessie Owen, 113; Mrs Frances Rogers Parry, 46; Miss Gwyneth Rees Roberts, 6, 7, 16, 18, 19, 21; Mrs Elsie Stanley, 30, 31; Mrs Anne Williams, 45, 120, 122, 123, 124, 126, 127, 128, 129; Mr Merfyn Williams, 26, 35; Gwynedd Archives Service, 9, 47; Gwynedd Library Service, 27, 34, 39, 43, 44, 53, 83, 89; The National Library of Wales, 4, 5, 72.

To all of them I should like to express my sincere thanks.

Finally, I hope that this second volume will stimulate interest in what life was like in Anglesey eighty or ninety years ago, and that it gives readers as much pleasure as I derived in compiling it.

Menai Bridge *John Cowell*
October 1992

INTRODUCTION

The Edwardian era began with the accession of Edward VII in 1901, following the death of his mother, Queen Victoria. Although the King died in 1910, the Edwardian period is generally regarded as having ended with the outbreak of the First World War in 1914, a natural watershed in British history. It was in many ways a period of transition. Britain's world economic supremacy was declining, foreign grain and meat were pouring into the country, and the British Empire had passed its peak of prosperity. A national system of elementary and secondary education was established, paid for out of the rates, and children were being medically examined at school. Death rates were falling rapidly and the expectancy of life was increasing. State pensions were introduced, and the National Insurance Act provided unemployment benefit and sick pay for the needy. Workers were organising themselves into unions, more leisure time became available, and seaside resorts were being opened up to the masses. Football and cricket were attracting large crowds, and the first £1,000 transfer fee for a footballer took place. Multiple shops were spreading throughout the country and introducing a wide range of branded goods at reduced prices. Technology was developing rapidly with the invention of the telephone, the gramophone, the typewriter and the box camera; Marconi sent messages across the Atlantic by wireless telegraphy, and Bleirot flew the Channel. Books and newspapers began to circulate freely, women's clothes became more stylish, and the cinema became a popular form of public entertainment. But possibly the greatest change which took place during the period was the development of the internal combustion engine. No other single influence since the Industrial Revolution made a greater impact on society, and by 1914 motor transport was plunging the country into a new era.

Yet in many ways life in Anglesey had changed little since late Victorian times. Agriculture was still the principal industry, with 40 per cent of the occupied male population working on the land, while almost a half of all women in employment were engaged in domestic service. There was no official age of retirement, three-quarters of all men over sixty-five were still in employment, and the elderly lived in constant fear of ending their days in the workhouse. Every village had a sprinkling of shops, the old rural crafts were still flourishing, and 92 per cent of the population spoke Welsh. Women were harshly exploited, found it impossible to obtain a divorce, and were not entitled to vote until 1918. Children were rigorously disciplined, made their own amusements, and could leave school at the age of twelve. Beer was twopence a pint, public houses were open sixteen hours a day, and the minimum drinking age was fourteen. Coal was a shilling a hundredweight, postage was still a penny, and a loaf could be bought for twopence. The average weekly wage was £1, a sixty-hour week was common, and leisure opportunities were few.

Sundays were joyless, sombre days, with no games or amusements, books or newspapers. People were deeply religious, and the middle classes were among the chapel's most stalwart supporters. A Royal Commission Report in 1910 estimated that 65 per cent of the population of Anglesey were members of the Nonconformist chapels, two-thirds of whom were Calvinistic Methodists, with another 9.5 per cent churchgoers. Furthermore, 75 per cent of all children under the age of fifteen attended Sunday School (59 per cent chapel and 16 per cent church), which helped to supplement the education they received during the week. The larger C.M. chapels held as many as ten services a week, so people's lives were inexorably bound up in their activities.

For the well-to-do the Edwardian period was an age of affluence and idleness, of peace and prosperity. Living in large country houses with a retinue of servants, with endless rounds of week-end parties, and interest on invested capital bringing a healthy return, the squirearchy were the classic symbols of a so-called 'golden age'.

Lower down the social order, those on incomes of £300 a year lived exceedingly well and had never had it so good. They could rent a detached house for £25 a year, fully furnish it for a little over £100 and employ a live-in maid for 5s. a week. Income tax was a shilling in the pound, a made-to-measure suit cost four guineas, a solid silver pocket watch 25s. and a bottle of whisky 3s.6d.

Yet for large numbers of the working class the Edwardian era was an age of profound misery and poverty. They were overworked, badly paid and undernourished, and lived in overcrowded conditions with inadequate sanitation and little knowledge of hygiene. Their predicament was made even worse by inflation, which pulled the real wages of the labouring poor below the poverty line and resulted in a marked deterioration in living standards. Food accounted for almost two-thirds of their meagre income, with little remaining for rent and clothing, and none for luxuries. At the base of the social pyramid were those unable to work through old age or infirmity. They were forced to seek the grudging help of the parish, and in some Anglesey villages as many as 20 per cent of the population were in receipt of outdoor relief. Begging in the streets was commonplace, and tramps were an intolerable nuisance.

The health of the Anglesey poor was appalling by modern standards, and without the resources to pay for medical care many suffered from ill-health throughout their lives. Teeth were hardly ever cleaned, except occasionally picked with a dead match, and when a school dental officer was appointed in Anglesey in 1913 he found that 83 per cent of those examined required several extractions or fillings. Children were vulnerable to all manner of diseases, and a national survey concluded that twelve-year-old working class boys were on average 5 inches shorter and 11 pounds lighter than boys of wealthier families.

Little attempt was made by politicians to redress the balance of inequality. Instead, wealth became more unevenly distributed, with the rich getting richer and the poor getting poorer. This resulted in a growing mood of unrest among the working classes, and a final confrontation between labour and capital was avoided only by the outbreak of war in August 1914. From then on everything changed and one of the most interesting periods of modern history came to an abrupt end.

A nostalgic view of Hill Street, Menai Bridge, just before the turn of the century, with a pedlar's donkey cart making its way slowly towards the Square. The whitewashed building on the left was the Cross Keys, a beerhouse kept by John Richard Jones, who also served tea and coffee in a back room. It was one of 18 licensed premises in Menai Bridge during the closing years of Victoria's reign before being demolished c.1896 to make way for the National Provincial Bank of England.

High Street, Menai Bridge, littered with horse-droppings, on a photograph taken at the turn of the century. There were three grocers and confectioners next door to one another at No. 40 (Lewis Jones), No. 42 (John Owens) and No. 44 (Owen Davies). The cottages on the left were later demolished and rebuilt, some of them as shops. It would appear that the entire population of the east end of the High Street, or Beaumaris Road as it was then called, had emerged to gaze curiously at the camera.

Medical Hall, Menai Bridge, in 1908, the imposing dispensary of Rees Roberts, who is seen in the photograph with his young son, Roland. As well as stocking a wide range of proprietary medicines it was common practice at this time for chemists to sell mineral waters, wines and tobacco. Rees Roberts was also a well-known photographer who produced some outstanding prints of local interest. In 1912 the premises were purchased by the London & Midland Bank and the pharmacy was re-located a few doors away in the High Street.

Mona House, Menai Bridge, a fashionable draper's shop, showing the annual winter sale in progress. This was a relatively new trading practice for disposing of unsold stock, and it provided the working class with an opportunity to purchase goods at genuinely reduced prices. One of the main features of the Edwardian era was the immense increase in the production of ready-made clothes, whose cheapness brought them within the range of all but the very poorest members of society. But middle and upper class families continued to have most of their clothes made by a tailor.

Menai Bridge Square, thronged with people and lined with stalls selling all manner of wares, on the occasion of the annual fair held on the 24th October each year. This was a great social event, eagerly awaited and saved for throughout the year by people who otherwise had little colour in their lives. There were peep shows, fortune tellers, coconut shies, roundabouts, boxing booths and Llanerchymedd 'Inja rock', all helping to make it a grand occasion. The imposing Post Office building was opened in June 1907 and this card was posted there four months later.

Bridge Street Stores, Menai Bridge, c. 1912, a high-class grocery shop owned by D.H. Pritchard, who had secured the business from Sophia Jones around the turn of the century. Its tightly packed but neatly arranged window display was the hallmark of a superior grocer, while the well-groomed staff in their clean white aprons and starched collars give the impression of efficiency and service. The business was taken over by J.H. Moss shortly after this photograph was taken and it remained in the family until his son, Mervyn, retired in 1988.

The Star Inn, Menai Bridge, one of four public houses in Water Street which catered for the drinking habits of the Edwardian working man. Miss Jane Hughes, the landlady, had taken over the licence from her father, who had held it since the opening of the tavern in the early 1840s. It must have been a thriving business in its early years as Hugh Hughes was able to afford two live-in servants in 1851.

The Liverpool Arms Hotel, Menai Bridge, in 1905. It was built in 1843 in order to cater for visitors landing from the Liverpool packets and for whom J.W. Thomas, the proprietor in 1910, was offering 'breakfasts, dinners and teas at moderate charges and a special week-end agreement'. The low building opposite the pier gates was a warehouse occupied by John Owen Edwards, a wholesale grocer, who was ideally situated to receive his supplies by sea. The old building was later demolished and a larger warehouse erected on the site.

The Bulkeley Arms, Menai Bridge in 1910, showing a horse-drawn cab owned by William Owen, a carriage proprietor of nearby Tan Rhiw. It was a family and commercial hotel run by J.T. Averill, who advertised that 'cyclists and visitors will find every comfort and attention at moderate charges'. Note the prominent gas lamp in the centre of the Square. Gas was supplied by the local gasworks and a lamplighter was employed by the council on a salary of £10 a year. Streets were not lit by electricity until 1913.

A peaceful scene on Menai Bridge promenade in 1910 as two horse-drawn cabs outside the Mostyn Arms await the arrival of the Liverpool steamer. The promenade was completed in 1904 at a cost of £1,564 and was officially opened, along with the extended pier, by David Lloyd George. The refreshment stall in the centre of the photograph was run by E.L. Williams, a confectioner of nearby Beach House, who rented the site from the council for £1.10s per season. Note the 'baby carriage' with its penny-farthing wheels. This was the popular style of the period and could be bought for £1.5s.

The Rock Vaults, Menai Bridge, in 1905. The public house was built in 1853 and during the early 1900s it was occupied by Ellis Timothy, who also ran a wholesale and bottling business in the town. The building was demolished in 1969 to make way for road improvements on one of the busiest highways in Anglesey, and was situated on what is now a large roundabout. The Anglesey Arms Hotel, before it was extensively altered, can be seen in the distance.

The weekly livestock sale at Menai Bridge c. 1910. Farmers and butchers, some of whom wear their best suits and bowler hats, mingle with each other before the serious business begins. Prior to the coming of motor transport animals were brought in by rail to Menai Bridge station and walked over the suspension bridge to the market place. The Smithfield was situated on a strip of land now occupied by Leo's store, and sales were conducted by John Pritchard, the Bangor auctioneer.

Eisteddfod Cadeiriol Môn, Porthaethwy. F.W.E.

The proclamation of the Anglesey Eisteddfod on Boncan Fawr, Menai Bridge, in 1912. The Eisteddfod itself was held on Whit Monday and Tuesday of the following year in a large marquee on the outskirts of the town and was preceded by the Gorsedd ceremony in the Square. Menai Bridge Band was in attendance and it subsequently won the brass band competition for a cup and £7 in prize money. A crowd of 3,000 was present at the Eisteddfod concert and the total attendance during the two days was over 10,000.

Menai Bridge Fire Brigade was established in 1898 when the Marquess of Anglesey presented the town with a horse-drawn manual fire-engine. This was replaced in 1911 by a Merryweather engine at a cost of £385, complete with 400 yards of hose, a rope escape and a jumping sheet. In order to accommodate the new engine a fire station was built in Dale Street the following year.
Standing (left to right): John Owen, John Hughes, R.J. Jones, Albert Rowlands, W. Morgan Jones, Owen Thomas (Captain).
Seated: J.R. Owen, Owen Evans, R.L. Williams.

Members of Menai Bridge Lawn Tennis Club photographed in the early 1900s alongside their court at Holyhead Road on the site now occupied by the telephone exchange. Lawn tennis originated in the mid-1870s, and after the first ladies final was played at Wimbledon in 1886 the game was taken up enthusiastically by women, even if they could only play with moderate exertion. Mixed sport also offered a screen for flirtation in an age when few other opportunities existed. It should be remembered that tennis, like golf, was a middle class game from which the lower orders were totally excluded.

A match in progress at the Menai Bridge Lawn Tennis Club after the official opening of a second court and wooden pavilion in May 1903. It was, of course, a private club, with annual subscriptions of 10s.6d for gentlemen and 7s.6d for ladies. Temporary membership was also available to visitors at 2s.6d per week, and a fine of 6d was imposed on anyone found playing in heeled boots. It is difficult nowadays to imagine how ladies could possibly play athletically in a hat, a high-collared blouse and a long sweeping skirt, but tennis at this time was a social rather than a competitive game.

A tranquil scene in Mount Street, Menai Bridge, in 1910, showing the Wesleyan Methodist chapel, erected in 1859 to replace the original meeting-house established on the site in 1831. A larger chapel was built at the lower end of Hill Street in 1902 on land now occupied by the Llys Tegla flats, and the old building has been used as the Menai Bridge band room ever since. The shop on the left was that of Thomas Pritchard, one of 11 grocers in the town at this time.

The woollen factory at Cadnant, Menai Bridge, c. 1910. Established during the 1840s it was run by John Morgan & Sons, and employed several weavers. Power was obtained from the River Cadnant, which was fed into a storage pond with sufficient head of water to drive a large wheel, but steam power was used whenever there was insufficient water available during long periods of dry weather. Cadnant was a hive of activity during the Edwardian era. In addition to the mill it housed a factory making writing-slates for schools, as well as a smithy and a shop.

Pupils at Llandegfan Council School c. 1905. Founded in 1727 and a former church school, it was brought under the control of the county council in 1902. The building in the photograph was erected in 1890 at a cost of £534, replacing an older one built in 1832. Teaching was monotonous and factual, with reliance on the repetitive learning of tables and rules of grammar. The teacher was paid an incremental salary of £85 to £110 a year. Some of the children wear ill-fitting clothes, probably handed down from other members of the family.

BISHOPS PALACE, GLYN GARTH.- ANGLESEY.

Glyn Garth, a magnificent mansion on the banks of the Menai Strait, built in 1850 at a cost of £40,000 by Salis Schwabe, a wealthy Manchester businessman of Swiss origin. But Mr Schwabe did not enjoy his new home for long as he died three years later. From 1900 to 1925 it became the official residence of Watkin Williams, the Bishop of Bangor, before being acquired by the Friendship Holidays Association. The house was demolished in 1964 to make way for a block of flats.

St Tudno (II), a handsome paddle steamer which plied daily between Liverpool and the Menai Strait each summer. Built in 1891 at a cost of £50,000 she was given the same name as the vessel she replaced. With accommodation for 1,061 passengers she brought thousands of holidaymakers to Anglesey during the Edwardian tourist boom for a second class return fare of 4s.6d. The *St Tudno* was sold in 1912 and broken up ten years later. A third steamer of the same name, and the one best remembered today, operated the Liverpool to Menai Bridge service from 1926 to 1962.

The paddle steamer *Snowdon* entering the Menai Strait in 1906. Built in 1892, with a speed of 14 knots and certified to carry 462 passengers, she ran regular excursions from Llandudno to the Menai Strait and Caernarfon, as well as cruises around Anglesey. The return fare to Beaumaris and Menai Bridge was 3s. first class and 2s. second class, while that to Caernarfon was an extra 1s. The *Snowdon* was sold by her owners in 1931 after 33 years of service in North Wales, during which time she had carried over half-a-million visitors through the Menai Strait.

Edward VII and the Royal party being entertained to afternoon tea on the terrace at Baron Hill on 9th July 1907, prior to the King laying the foundation stone of the new University College building at Bangor.
Standing: H.R. Hughes of Kinmel, Lord Tweedmouth.
Seated (left to right): Sir Richard Bulkeley, Queen Alexandra, Lady Magdalen Bulkeley, Edward VII, Miss Siriol Bulkeley, Princess Victoria, the Countess of Gosford.

A hunt meeting at Baron Hill c. 1910. Hunting was the prerogative of the gentry as a pack of hounds cost an enormous sum to maintain. But invitations to participate were extended to others, and these were eagerly sought after by those aspiring to county status. Another favourite pastime of the well-to-do was shooting, and some astonishing bags are recorded. 7 guns shot 355 pheasants in a day's shoot at Bodorgan and 332 at Trescawen, while in a three-months season no fewer than 2,074 pheasants, 554 partridges and 442 rabbits were accounted for at Parciau, Plas Gwyn and Bodorgan.

Sir Richard Bulkeley's new motor car, a 20 h.p. Argyle, registered in March 1906, with the number EY 1 retained from a previous vehicle. It was the ultimate symbol of wealth and status, expensive to buy and costly to run. Tyres needed replacing every 700 miles or so and punctures were a constant problem on the untarred roads of the period. Powerful cars used almost as much oil as petrol and there were very few garages able to cope with a breakdown. Fuel costs were the cheapest item. Petrol was 1s.6d a gallon but increased in 1909 by a tax of 3d.

CHAPEL STREET. BEAUMARIS. W+CO.

Most of the houses seen on this 1910 postcard of Chapel Street, Beaumaris, were owned by the Baron Hill Estate. The whitewashed cottages on the right were rented for 1s.6d a week and in 1920 they were sold by auction, along with 237 other properties in the town belonging to the Estate. Three of the cottages were purchased by the Beaumaris & District Motor Company and were demolished to make way for a garage. The sign on the left reads: 'Liverpool Arms Stables. Carriages for hire'.

A splendid display of meat at John Stanley's shop in Beaumaris, with the proprietor and his son (in the white apron) standing proudly outside. John Stanley was previously in business in Market Place, and later in Wexham Street, before moving to Castle Street in 1909 to the building which formerly housed the Allen Public Library. He was one of five butchers in Beaumaris at this time and he also had branches in Llangoed and Penmon. The business remained in the family until the retirement of Wilfred and Elsie Stanley in 1984.

Heavy traffic in Castle Street, Beaumaris, a scene which would bring chaos to today's traffic but which was a common sight during Edwardian times. Cattle and sheep were walked from Menai Bridge Smithfield to the town abattoir in Wexham Street, where John Stanley advertised that his animals were 'slaughtered with the R.S.P.C.A's humane killer'. Yet conditions in the abattoir were deplorable, with blood running freely into the town drains, and it was not until 1913 that the Borough Council intervened to reduce the health risk.

A hackney carriage picking up a well-dressed passenger near the pier entrance at Beaumaris in 1909. The carriage had a capacity to carry 4 passengers but its metal tyres must have given them an uncomfortable ride. There were 24 hackney carriages and drivers licensed by the Borough Council at this time, a third of them being held by the firm of Williams Brothers of the Bull's Head Horse and Carriage Repository, before it went out of business in 1911. The fare to Bangor was 1s.6d and to Menai Bridge 1s.

A group of children playing happily on the beach alongside the pier at Beaumaris in 1908, in the days before the pollution of the Menai Strait put an end to such activities. The girls all wear large bonnets to shelter their faces from the sun because the Edwardians, like the Victorians before them, believed that sun-tanned skin was a degrading feature in a woman. There were strict bye-laws governing bathing in Beaumaris: 'No person, unless effectively screened from view, shall bathe from the sea-shore without wearing suitable drawers or other sufficient covering to prevent indecent exposure of his person'.

A steam-driven Clayton & Shuttleworth threshing machine at work on a farm near Beaumaris during the early 1900s. This took much of the toil out of threshing but was well beyond the means of all but the largest farmers. The common practice was for such expensive machinery to be hired from a firm of steam contractors, such as Rowland Thomas of Llanbedrgoch, and at prices they could afford. Harvesting was the busiest time of the agricultural year and involved taking on extra hands, who worked from dawn until dusk as long as the weather held.

Beaumaris Fire Brigade, resplendent in new helmets and uniforms supplied by the Borough Council in 1905. The firemen were all volunteers and were paid a shilling for attending the monthly fire drill, as well as loss of earnings when on fire duty. Owners of properties which caught fire were charged £2.2s. for a call-out, while those outside the town paid £5.5s. The fire engine was horse-drawn and had a coal-burning boiler, seen at the rear end, which produced sufficient steam for pumping up to 250 gallons of water a minute.

CHURCH STREET & POST OFFICE, BEAUMARIS.

Beaumaris Post Office in 1910. It was built in 1908 to replace the old Castle Street premises which were inadequate to cope with the rapid growth in business that had taken place during the closing years of Victoria's reign. The *North Wales Chronicle* greeted its opening with enthusiasm, describing the office as "surpassing any other building of similar capacity in Wales both in convenience and solidity of construction". The sub-postmaster was John Owen Jones who had been appointed in 1900 on a salary of £84 a year. He had an establishment of 8 postmen, 2 telegram boys, 2 sorting clerks and 2 telegraphists.

A detachment of troops from Kingsbridge Camp, Llanfaes, photographed outside Beaumaris Castle before being drafted to France during the First World War. Inspired to volunteer by patriotism and the adventure of war they had little idea of the horrors awaiting them in the trenches, where one in every five of those who served there would not return. Included in these figures were 950 young Anglesey men, as witnessed by the war memorials erected in every town and village in the county.

ON THE ROAD TO LLANGOED COTTAGES, LLANFAES, ANGLESEY. W & CO.

A peaceful scene at Llanfaes, on the road between Llangoed and Beaumaris, as a pony and trap makes its way slowly towards the camera. The postcard was written by a holidaymaker in 1910 and bears the message: *'Having a lovely time. Llangoed is absolutely it'.* The row of cottages, known locally as Tai Lôn Dre, are still standing today, and apart from the absence of traffic and some road widening, the scene has changed little in over eighty years.

38

Haymaking on a Llanfaes farm c. 1910, using a mower with a moveable side cutting bar. This speeded up the operation and removed much of the drudgery from the task, although the remaining processes of raking and stacking were usually done by hand. Grass mowers, which had been developed before 1850, were exhibited at local agricultural shows by the leading manufacturers such as Ransomes, Sims and Jefferies, and were becoming popular with Anglesey farmers. But on small holdings hay was still cut by hand during the years leading up to the First World War.

Mona Terrace, Llangoed, in 1909, with a group of children standing in the middle of the road safe in the knowledge that they would not be run over. Llangoed was a typical Anglesey village, with a population of 960, and almost completely self-sufficient. It boasted 5 grocers, 2 general stores, 2 bakers and confectioners, a tobacconist, a butcher, a glass and china dealer, a draper, a tailor, a dressmaker and 4 carriage proprietors. Mona Terrace was built in 1897 and was known familiarly as Lôn Refail.

A lady cyclist poses for the camera in Llangoed c. 1910. Cycling had become a popular leisure pastime since the late eighties, when the chain-driven 'safety' bicycle had replaced the 'penny farthing' and Dunlop had invented the pneumatic tyre. It had also become a socially acceptable form of recreation for women as the 'safety' bicycle enabled them to ride in long skirts, especially when fitted with a guard over the rear wheel. The craze reached its height during the Edwardian era, and by 1914 there were over three million bicycles on British roads. Mass production methods brought prices tumbling down. In 1900 'Mona' cycles were advertised in the local press for £12, but by 1914 three-speed models were offered at £5.5s. A good second-hand machine could be bought for £1, which proved to be a cheap form of transport for work and for pleasure for all but the poorest families. Most villages had a cycle agent who also undertook repairs, and many hotels offered cheap accommodation for members of cycling clubs.

Penmon Marble Quarry in 1912. It had produced the stone for building the Menai and Conway bridges, Holyhead harbour and the Marquess of Anglesey's column at Llanfairpwll, and by the turn of the century its products were much in demand by the construction industry. There were two other quarries in Penmon, Dinmor and Flagstaffe, which produced limestone for building work and for the manufacture of stematic pig iron. Between them the three quarries employed 200 men before the First World War and had an average annual output of some 150,000 tons, much of it being shipped to distant markets.

The Penmon lifeboat, apparently in difficulties on the newly built slipway, on a calm day during the early 1900s. She was the *Christopher Brown*, built in 1896 at a cost of £514, and the third Penmon lifeboat of that name. The station had been open since 1832 but was closed in 1915 when a larger one was established at Beaumaris. During her nineteen years' service at Penmon the *Christopher Brown* was launched on average once a year and saved a total of 45 lives.

A father and his two feeble-minded children, who were believed to have lived in Penmon during the early 1900s. The 1871 Census was the first to include questions on lunacy, and that of 1911 enumerated 44 imbeciles and 68 feeble-minded persons in Anglesey, 9 of whom were under the age of fifteen. After the death of their parents mentally handicapped children were likely to end up in the workhouse, where they were generally welcomed as useful servants because of the lack of able-bodied inmates to undertake the household chores. Only those believed to be dangerous were assigned to the lunatic asylum. Other disabilities which reduced people's chances of supporting themselves were included in the 1911 Census for Anglesey. 39 were listed as deaf and dumb, 19 totally deaf and 37 blind. It is quite remarkable that this photograph was ever taken, as those suffering from mental deficiency were usually hidden away from prying eyes.

Penmynydd Post Office was opened on the 1st September 1902 in Elizabeth Jones's grocery shop at Pant Mawr, and it carried an annual salary of £6.11s. before being increased to £9 when Perry Owen took over in 1907. Penmynydd was dependent on LLanfairpwll for its mail, which was carried there by William Jones, a rural auxiliary, who was paid 13s.10d a week plus a shilling for the maintenance of his bicycle. On passing the Civil Service examination in 1909 he was appointed as an established postman and his wages increased to 21s.

A train stops at Pentraeth, a single platform halt on the Red Wharf Bay Railway, while its crew find time to pose for the camera. The branch line was opened as far as Pentraeth on 1st July 1908 and was completed to its terminus on 24th May the following year, with an intermediate halt at Llanbedrgoch. It had a passenger service of five trains a day in each direction, with an extra one on Thursdays, as well as a daily goods train. The station was closed to passenger traffic on 22nd September 1930.

Mary Elizabeth Parry and John, her husband, with their three young children and Nel, the maid, stand proudly in the doorway of their grocery shop in Pentraeth. Mary Parry had taken over the shop from her father, Thomas Rogers, who had been sub-postmaster there from 1881 to 1900. Known locally as 'Hen Bost', the shop can be traced back to 1767, and from humble beginnings it developed into a thriving concern during the nineteenth century. Despite the shop's uninviting appearance the Parry family continued to run a successful business during the Edwardian years. The building was demolished in 1982.

The Glanrafon Hotel, Benllech, on a postcard written by a resident and posted in 1910. The hotel was built during the 1870s when seaside holidays were becoming popular among the middle classes and Benllech was beginning to attract fashionable visitors. Lit by acetylene gas the hotel boasted 'a tennis lawn, a billiard room, hot and cold baths, a special sanitary certificate and the latest interior design'. The novelist Arnold Bennett and the French composer Claude Debussy were reported to have stayed there during the Edwardian era, when the inclusive terms were 10s.6d a day and £3.13s.6d a week.

Children from a well-to-do family in Benllech pose for the camera with their favourite dolls. Manufactured toys were plentiful for those who could afford them, and good quality British-made dolls could be bought for 3s.6d. The girls in the photograph no doubt had a nanny, hired for £20 to £30 a year, and a nursery crammed with expensive toys, games and books. Those of the poor, on the other hand, made their own amusement and were lucky if they had a home-made rag doll, a skipping rope and the occasional toy procured from a penny bazaar.

Thomas David Hughes of Bodlondeb, Talwrn, at the wheel of his new car outside Regent House, Bridge Street, Llangefni, a well-known outfitters shop, now demolished. It was a four-seater 8 h.p. MMC (Motor Manufacturing Company) with wooden wheels, solid tyres, tiller steering and acetylene lamps, and first registered in March 1904 as EY 29. These early cars were generally unreliable, with frequent breakdowns and few country garages capable of diagnosing the faults. The bemused children seem unsure which is the more exciting novelty, the car or the camera.

The Parliamentary Election of January 1910, when Ellis Jones Griffith, a Liberal, was returned as Member for Anglesey after defeating R.O. Roberts, the Conservative candidate. The postcard shows Ellis Jones Griffith seated in the car, with the Rev John Williams, Brynsiencyn, standing alongside and about to drive away under the watchful eye of the law. The car, a 10 h.p. two-seater Zedel, registered EY 89, was owned by John Morris Jones. The January election was followed by a major constitutional crisis, caused by the House of Lords rejecting Lloyd George's 'People's Budget' and resulting in another election eleven months later, when Ellis Jones Griffith was returned unopposed.

Dicks shoeshop at 14 High Street, Llangefni, c. 1910. This was one of the first multiples to be established in the area, with branches at Amlwch, Holyhead and Bangor. It boasted 'the largest stock in Anglesey', and the prices of its factory-made footwear were lower than those of traditional shoemakers. Mass production by machinery and new trading techniques enabled the firm to offer ladies 'K' shoes at 2s.11d, ladies button boots at 3s.11d and gents 'Holdfast' boots at 4s.11d, all noted for 'easy fitting in the latest styles'.

An impressive display of meat hanging outside the shop of Richard Jones & Son at 30 High Street, Llangefni, a normal practice adopted by butchers in pre-refrigeration times. The meat had to be disposed of within a few days and was often sold off cheaply on a Saturday night. Prices depended on seasonal variation and on quality, with beef and pork averaging 8d a lb in 1907 and home-killed lamb 9d. There were five other butchers in Llangefni at this time so Richard Jones had to rely on quality and service in order to attract custom.

Betsy Jones's delivery van, driven by John Jones and drawn by a handsome-looking horse, on its daily round in Llangefni c. 1905. This was a popular style of closed baker's cart because of its ample headroom and internal sliding trays for ease of loading. It was probably custom built by Hugh Hughes of Church Street, one of the largest coach builders in Anglesey during the early 1900s. The owner's name is attractively displayed on the side and it gives the general appearance of cleanliness. Miss Betsy Jones was a high-class baker and confectioner who was also the proprietress of the Gwalia Temperance Hotel in Bridge Street.

The entrance to the goods yard at Llangefni railway station after a heavy fall of snow, possibly during the winter of 1907-08, when Anglesey experienced two severe snowstorms. Many areas were brought to a standstill and the freezing conditions enabled children to skate safely on Llyn Pwmp. Despite the treacherous conditions it appeared to be 'business as usual' for the coal carrier. This was one of a number of superb photographs taken by Maurice Price showing various views of Llangefni covered with a blanket of snow.

Market day at Llangefni c.1910, with Maurice Price's 'Shop Station' on the left. Price was a professional photographer who produced prints of fine quality at a time when camera equipment was cumbersome and exposure times relatively long. He also published picture postcards of local views which have survived as an invaluable record of what life was like in Anglesey eighty or ninety years ago. Maurice Price was one of two professional photographers in Llangefni during the early 1900s, the other being T.H. Hughes, a specialist in studio portraits, who also had a shop in the High Street.

The hiring fair at Llangefni c. 1910. This was held in May and November each year when labourers and female servants seeking employment had to suffer the indignity of standing like cattle in the market place to await the inspection of the farmers. Wages were settled by individual bargaining, which invariably worked to the advantage of the farmer, and once sealed by a handshake the worker was tied to his employer for six or twelve months. Although widely condemned as a degrading form of slave market, hiring fairs continued to function until after the First World War.

A familiar scene outside the Red Lion public house in Llangefni High Street eighty or ninety years ago. No one seemed concerned about the congestion that may have been caused as livestock markets had always been held in the main thoroughfare, but hygiene regulations and the coming of motor transport forced them to move to an enclosed site behind the High Street. The photographer has timed his exposure to perfection as it shows the two farmers on the right sealing a bargain with a handshake.

The presence of the camera was still sufficiently unusual in 1910 to hold up the sale of sheep at Llangefni Smithfield. This was located on a strip of land behind Dicks shop in the High Street after a council bye-law had prohibited the sale of livestock in the streets. When a larger Smithfield was later opened by H.T. Owen, a Church Street auctioneer, the old site was used as a storage yard by Hughes, Gray & Company, ironmongers and implement merchants, before being built upon.

Berni's mobile chipped potato wagon at Llangefni c. 1910. Known locally as 'Joe Chips' he toured the district with his horse-drawn vehicle before eventually opening a shop in Bridge Street and introducing fried fish on the menu. Chipped potatoes were a novelty in Anglesey during the early 1900s, although they had been sold by street traders in London and the Lancashire towns since 1880. Berni's main customers were ordinary working people, who saw this exciting new delicacy as a welcome relief from their normal monotonous diet.

The London Missionary Society's touring caravan at Llangefni c. 1910. The smart appearance and artificial pose of the children suggest that they were carefully chosen to emphasise the necessity of fundraising for the spreading of Christianity abroad. This was an important activity in the chapels, particularly at Sunday schools, where lantern-slides and talks by visiting missionaries helped to fund the movement. It was well-supported at Llangefni, where over 80 per cent of the population were members of Nonconformist chapels in 1910. Over 53 per cent attended Sunday school, with just under half of these being under the age of fifteen.

Some of the poor inhabitants of Llangefni waiting for soup to be distributed at Mona Cafe during the early 1900s. This was organised and funded by middle class ladies with time on their hands who regarded private charity as a normal humanitarian responsibility. There was a great deal of poverty in Llangefni during the Edwardian era, much of which was attributed to unemployment, and an average of 75 families were in receipt of outdoor parish relief in 1914. This represented almost 7 per cent of the town population, compared with a figure of 2.5 per cent for North Wales as a whole.

A rare glimpse of a working-class wedding in Llangefni c. 1910. Despite their poverty, some of the guests appear to be respectably dressed for the occasion, but the gentleman standing next to the bride still wears his working trousers and gaiters. Weddings, like the lives of the lower order, were colourless and sober, with little ceremony, few gifts and no honeymoon. They were held on a Saturday afternoon and the groom would be back at work on the following Monday. Unlike well-to-do parents, who carefully vetted all would-be suitors, those of the poor were only too pleased to see their daughters taken off their hands.

A steam-powered threshing machine at work on a Llangefni farm during the early 1900s. This was generally hired from a steam contractor as the cost of purchase could only be justified on large farms, and there were not many of these in Anglesey. In fact 78 per cent of all holdings were less than 50 acres, with a further 11 per cent between 50 and 100 acres. A mere 20 farms, or 0.5 per cent, had over 300 acres. The majority of farmers were tenants, and only 7 per cent of the occupants owned their own land.

A photographer was quickly on the scene of this road accident at Nant Gate, near Llangefni, during the early years of motoring. It was, perhaps, one of the first car accidents on Anglesey roads, and was unusual enough to attract a large crowd of curious onlookers. Unfortunately the postcard is undated and, surprisingly, no report of the incident can be found in the local press. However, the message on the reverse side of the card reads: *'Dyma i chwi llun motor accident nos Sadwrn yn Nant Gate'.*

Ebenezer chapel at Cildwrn, Llangefni, commonly known as Christmas Evans's chapel, in 1905. Built originally in 1781 this was the first Baptist chapel in Anglesey. It was demolished in 1814 to make way for a larger building and was completely renovated in 1846. Christmas Evans (1766-1838) was a self-taught son of a Cardiganshire shoemaker, and his tireless evangelism did much to spread the Baptist gospel in Anglesey. The building still stands on the outskirts of the town and is now an Evangelical church.

LLANGEFNI.- Town Hall, Memorial Chapel & County Buildings.

New Year Greetings

Picture postcards were widely used as Christmas cards and New Year cards during Edwardian times, and those with local views were often embossed with festive greetings, in both Welsh and English. They were popular with people of limited means as they could be bought for a penny each, compared with the more expensive traditional cards, and sent through the post for $^1/_2$d. This card was published by E. Williams of nearby Caxton House and was posted in Llangefni at 7.45 p.m. on the 31st December 1911 for guaranteed delivery in Menai Bridge the following day.

Cefni Hospital, funded by the Edward VII Welsh National Memorial Association, was officially opened in June 1915 after £5,500 had been collected within the county towards the building costs. Accommodation was provided for 24 patients suffering from tuberculosis, a grievous killer which accounted for one death in every nine in the rural districts of Anglesey in 1912. There was no known cure, but with rest and a good diet the disease could be arrested if diagnosed early enough. The poor could not afford hospital treatment so they were left to die at home or in the workhouse infirmary.

The visit of a street photographer seemed to attract a great deal of curiosity at Bodffordd, where life had changed little since mid-Victorian times, apart from the appearance of the motor car seen outside the post office. This was a five-seater 20 h.p. Ford, registered EY 827, and owned by Richard Hughes. He was one of three grocers in Bodffordd, as well as being the village sub-postmaster, having succeeded Katherine Parry on a salary of £19.5s a year. For outdoor work he had the assistance of a part-time postman who earned 9s. a week for delivering the mail as far as Bodala.

Llangwyllog station was opened in 1866 as an intermediate one on the Anglesey Central Railway, and a new building was erected in 1882. Apart from Holland Arms, which was the junction for the Red Wharf branch, Llangwyllog was the only station on the line which had a passing place and two platforms. In 1908 there were 16 passenger trains stopping there each weekday, 8 in each direction, with an extra one on market day. The line was finally closed to passenger traffic on 5th December 1964.

Llanerchymedd station on the Anglesey Central Railway, which was built with stone from nearby quarries and opened in 1866. The single-track line was completed to the terminus at Amlwch the following year. The only serious accident on the line occurred about a mile north of Llanerchymedd on 29th November 1877, when a bridge collapsed after a dam at nearby Pandy mill had been breached. The early morning train from Gaerwen plunged into the swollen River Alaw, killing the driver, the stoker and a ganger.

A cattle fair in the High Street, Llanerchymedd, from a photograph by John Thomas (1838-1905), showing the lost atmosphere of a once familiar scene long since vanished. This was the main thoroughfare through the town but to the farmers it was the rightful place to buy and sell, or merely to stand and gossip. Cattle were brought in by rail or were walked there before the coming of motor transport. Fairs were held at Llanerchymedd once a month but specialised ones for cattle took place in May and October each year.

A large crowd, accompanied by the local brass band, gathers in the Square, Llanerchymedd, for the proclamation of the Anglesey Eisteddfod in 1910. This was held on Whit Monday and Tuesday of the following year and the event proved to be a resounding success. Admission receipts and donations amounted to £623, which left a substantial surplus of income over expenditure. The winner of the chair was Elfyn, the well-known bard from Blaenau Ffestiniog.

Rhosgoch station on the last stretch of the Anglesey Central Railway. It was opened in 1867 and new buildings were erected in 1882 to replace the original wood shed. It was intended to construct a branch line from Rhosgoch to Cemaes and from there to Valley to connect with the main Holyhead line, but the plan never materialised because of financial difficulties. Rhosgoch was a busy country station during Edwardian times and was used extensively by local farmers for transporting livestock and agricultural produce.

THE SQUARE, NEBO VILLAGE,
NEAR LLANEILIAN BAY.

A peaceful scene in the tiny village of Nebo in 1910. The Bull's Head public house can be seen at the end of the Square, with Elizabeth Parry, the licensee, standing near the doorway. This was closed in 1919. Next door to the Bull is Mary Jones's grocery shop, one of two in the village at this time, a surprising number for such a small community, especially as Penysarn, with no fewer than eight grocers, was only half-a-mile away.

The message on this postcard of Amlwch Port, posted there on the 20th August 1911, describes the labour unrest which threatened to bring the country to a standstill in the summer of that year when miners, railwaymen, seamen and dockers all took industrial action. Over a million workers were involved and more than ten million working days were lost. It reads: *'The port of Amlwch is almost deserted now because of the sailors' strike. Isn't the railway stoppage dreadful? We dare not go by train in case we cannot get back.'*

The windmill at Amlwch Port in 1906. Built in 1816 for John Paynter it was one of the largest mills in Anglesey, having four storeys and the capacity to grind 70 bushels of corn per hour. In addition to grinding on commission for local farmers, Paynter was also an independent corn merchant who shipped supplies to distant markets. But once imported grain started flooding into the country and large roller mills became established at the main ports of entry, the days of the Anglesey windmills were over.

Amlwch Square in 1905, with the Dinorben Hotel on the right. The large gas lamp, one of 43 in the town in 1904, was lit only from October to March at a cost of a shilling a week. It was extinguished at 11 pm each weekday and at 9 pm on Sundays, as well as during moonlight nights. Surprisingly, the town was not supplied with electricity until 1936, whereas the street lamps of Holyhead had been converted 32 years earlier. The postcard bears a relevant message: *'What do you think of our village lamp? It's a bit of hot stuff.'*

A quiet scene outside Amlwch Post Office c. 1912. It had been established in 1826 at the King's Head inn, and during the next eighty years it was housed at three different locations - Methusalem Street, Petters Street and Mona Street. In 1907 the office achieved Crown status and moved to the existing building, leased from John Jones, a local cornmerchant, for £40 p.a. Owen Dew, the sub-postmaster, had an establishment of 3 clerks, a telegraphist, 11 postmen and 2 telegram boys. The office served a wide area, with rural postmen delivering as far as Bull Bay, Llys Dulas, Llaneilian, Tynrefail and Tyddyn Barma.

Salem Street, Amlwch, c. 1910, with a solitary coal wagon owned by Owen Hughes, a local carrier, the only vehicle in sight. Coal retailed at a shilling a hundredweight and was originally shipped to Amlwch Port, but when freight rates were undercut by the L.N.W.R. much of it was brought in by rail. The shop with the large window near the coal wagon was known as Railway Stores and was run by Owen Thomas, a tea and provision dealer, the popular name for a grocer in Edwardian times.

An Amlwch milkman on his daily round c. 1910. Milk carts were light, two-wheeled vehicles with a low floor line to enable the heavy churns to be loaded easily and for the driver to stand at the rear. Prior to being sold in bottles milk was supplied direct from the churn into the customer's jug by means of a measuring can, and the regular delivery of fresh milk was an essential service in pre-refrigeration days. The price of milk was subject to seasonal variation but it averaged 2d a pint during the Edwardian era.

NUMBER | TELEGRAMS "HILLS, AMLWCH" | ESTABLISHED 1840. | CHEMICAL MANURE WORKS.

39030

AMLWCH 30 May 1906

ANGLESEY, NORTH WALES.

R. C. Harding Esq. Vaynol Ck. Pt. Dinorwic

BOUGHT OF HENRY HILLS & SON.

Terms: .... | .... per Ton discount for Prompt Cash, or
.... | .... ,, ,, ,, Cash in 3 Months .... *Agent.*
or Nett Cash in 6 Months, (Interest charged on Overdue Accounts).

An attractive billhead of Henry Hills & Son, Chemical Manure Works, Amlwch. Established in 1840, the firm produced artificial fertilizers of many kinds, from nitro-phosphate and bone compound to superphosphate and Peruvian Guano. These were advertised widely, and with 27 agents throughout North Wales the firm's products were much in demand by farmers. The works were located on the site now occupied by the Associated Octel Company.

Workers employed by Edward Morgan & Company, the largest of three tobacco and snuff manufacturers in Amlwch during the early 1900s. The firm's celebrated 'Amlwch shag', which sold for 4d an ounce, was a household name throughout North Wales, as was its 'Snowdon mixture', 'Pride of Wales', 'Limerick roll', 'Workman's friend', 'Ladies twist', 'Yr Hen Wlad' and 'Baco'r Aelwyd'. Edward Morgan also took advantage of the estimated eight-fold increase in cigarette smoking, especially among women, which took place between 1895 and 1914, with branded packets of twenty selling for 3d.

An exhibition of pupils' work at Amlwch Elementary School in March 1914. When responsibility for education was transferred from school boards to the county council in 1902 the curriculum was widened to include practical subjects, such as sewing and craftwork, and the exhibits on view appear to dispel the myth that teaching consisted entirely of the three Rs. Note the wording on the blackboards, which are written in English only, despite the fact that 95 per cent of the population of Amlwch was Welsh-speaking at this time. The two teachers in the photograph are Miss Mary Jones, the infants headmistress, and Miss Jinny Hughes.

Amlwch station, the terminus of the Anglesey Central Railway, which was opened in 1867. The original wooden structure was rebuilt in 1884 with the addition of a waiting room, a lamp room, an extended covered platform and a locomotive shed. A planned extension to Amlwch Port was abandoned because of a lack of capital. The Railway Company was, in fact, in serious financial difficulties, owing £40,000 to its debenture holders and £12,000 in interest, so in 1876 it was sold to the L.N.W.R.

Seaman William Williams, V.C., D.S.M. & bar, M.M. (1890-1965), being presented with a gold watch in his home town of Amlwch in 1918. He was awarded the Victoria Cross for conspicuous bravery at sea for his part in the sinking of a German submarine (*UC 29*) whilst serving as a gunner on H.M.S. *Pargust*, a decoy ship disguised as a merchant vessel. He was also given a hero's welcome at Llangefni, where he was presented with an illuminated address and National War Bonds to the value of £120.

A large crowd, accompanied by the town band, gathers outside the Eleth Hotel, Amlwch, to celebrate the end of the First World War in November 1918. The horrors of the 'war to end all wars' had resulted in the most tragic casualty list ever known. Almost three-quarters of a million British soldiers had been killed and over two million injured, the cream of the country. Amlwch alone had lost 61 of its finest young men, and many of those who did return suffered from disabilities of some kind for the rest of their lives.

Amlwch, Bull Bay.

Bull Bay lifeboat station was opened in 1867 and a boathouse built the following year for £158. This was replaced in 1904 by a larger boathouse with a roller slipway at a cost of £2,000 in order to accommodate a new lifeboat, the *James Cullen*. The station was closed by the R.N.L.I. in 1926 and during its 58 years of service it had been involved in the rescue of 63 lives. This postcard of 1910, published by C.H. Smith of Bull Bay, shows the new boathouse, with the old one in the distance.

The Cemaes lifeboat *George Evans*, which was brought into service in 1887. She remained at Cemaes until 1907, when she was replaced by the *Charles Henry Ashley*, and during her twenty years' stay there she was called out 31 times and saved 3 lives. The Cemaes station had been opened in 1872 and a boathouse built there for £182, but a larger one was constructed in 1907 at a cost of £3,840. Several heroic rescues were recorded over the years, but after a steady fall in the number of calls on the lifeboat the station was closed in 1932.

Cemaes Bay High Street, previously known as Post Office Place, in 1905. This was a perfectly safe place for a small boy to stand in the days before motor transport disrupted the tranquility of village life. With a population of 971 Cemaes at this time had 5 grocers, 2 butchers, a baker, a draper, a chemist, a hairdresser and an ironmonger. The shop on the left with the sign above the door was that of W. Pritchard, a basket maker. This postcard was published by O.R. Morris of Stanley Studio, a well-known local photographer.

Glan Rhyd, Cemaes, seen on a postcard dated 8th September 1914. Although the country was already at war people were still taking holidays, as is clear from the message on the reverse side of the card: *'This is a view of the only boarding house in Cemaes that can take you at present'.* A week's stay at Glan Rhyd could be had for as little as £1 per head, a sum generally affordable by the better-off among the working class, such as white-collar workers with an income of £100 a year and a fortnight's paid holiday.

The Cemaes rural postman on the Cemlyn and Simdda Wen round, with Tanrallt seen in the distance. During the early 1900s this was a walking round, but by the time this photograph was taken in 1906 a mailcart had been supplied. As a part-time auxiliary the postman earned 7s. a week for a split shift of about four hours a day. The mail was carried by rail to Amlwch and from thence to Cemaes by wagonette, hired from T.O. Jones of the Vigour Inn for 10s. a week.

Wylfa Hall, Cemaes, built in 1880 by David Hughes (1820-1904). He was a local man who, after serving an apprenticeship as a joiner at Llanfechell, went to Liverpool to seek work before eventually becoming one of the largest builders in the city and amassing considerable wealth. In 1898 he erected a large village institute at Cemaes, at a cost of £2,500, and donated it to the local community. Whilst still retaining his Liverpool home, David Hughes spent most of the summer months at Wylfa Hall. It was demolished in 1971 when work commenced on the construction of the nuclear power station.

A typical town centre scene during the early 1900s as a policeman keeps an eye on the children in Stanley Street, Holyhead, which was evidently a place to stand and gossip before motor traffic transformed town and country alike. There was little to occupy the children during the school holidays and there were numerous complaints to the police, through the columns of the local press, about the nuisance caused by boys playing football in the streets of Holyhead, whose 'conduct and language are a disgrace'.

Stallholders and shoppers line up for the camera outside Holyhead market on a Saturday in 1904. Built in 1855 at a cost of £3,000 and carefully regulated by the council, the market played an important part in the economic life of the town, where consumers were able to satisfy most of their needs in food, clothing and household goods. Note the portable fryer on the left of the postcard, from which the vendor sold chips, a delicacy popularised by the working class. Three years later a 'chip potato saloon' was opened in the town, the first to be established in Anglesey.

Holyhead.   *S-S. 9/12/03*   *Boston Street.*

Williams, Boston House, Holyhead.

A horse and gig pulls up outside Medical Hall, Holyhead, in 1903. This was the flourishing shop of R.H. Williams, who had taken over the business from Theophilus Roberts a few years earlier. He offered the hypochondriac Edwardians all manner of proprietary medicines for the 'certain cure' of gout, lumbago, rheumatism, toothache, stomach disorders, eczema, kidney complaints and chest infections. The shop of Emma Williams, bookseller, stationer and postcard publisher, is seen next door at Boston House.

Holyhead Post Office in 1912. The office had been moved from Stanley Street to this newly acquired site in Boston Street ten years earlier, and the *Caernarvon Herald* described its opening as 'an event of unusual importance in the history of the town'. Opening hours were from 8.00 am to 7.30 pm on weekdays and from 8.30 am to 10.00 am on Sundays, bank holidays and Christmas Day. There were three deliveries of mail in the town each day - at 7.00 am, 2.40 pm and 5.15 pm

County Schools, Holyhead

Holyhead was the third county school to be established in Anglesey after Beaumaris (1895) and LLangefni (1897). It opened in 1901 in temporary accommodation in the town, with 19 pupils and R. Pugh Jones as Headmaster. Two years later the roll had increased to 52, with a staff of 3, and a new building was erected at a cost of £400, consisting of eight classrooms and a chemistry laboratory. By 1908 the number of pupils had increased to 160 so two new rooms were added for £442 and playing fields obtained at a rental of £9 a year.

HOLYHEAD STATION - EASY TRANSFER, TRAIN & STEAMER.

Holyhead station was built with a platform on each side of the harbour so that passengers could step straight from the steamer to the train, and vice-versa. The L.N.W.R. provided an excellent service, and in 1908 there were six through trains per day to and from Euston to connect with the Irish boats. Full catering facilities were provided on all trains, with sleeping saloons available on the Night Express. Return fares from London to Holyhead were £3.15s. first class and £1.15s.6d third class. Through tickets to Dublin could also be purchased from as little as £2.0s.6d.

The inner harbour at Holyhead in 1908, showing two L.N.W.R. express steamers lying at the departure (left) and arrival berths. The harbour was a busy place at this time, with no fewer than 7 steamers leaving Holyhead each day and an equal number arriving. There were 2 passenger and 2 cargo services to Dublin, a passenger-cargo run to Greenore, all operated by the L.N.W.R., plus 2 passenger services on the City of Dublin Company's mailboats. The clock in the foreground was erected to commemorate the opening of the new harbour and station complex by the Prince of Wales in 1880.

The express passenger steamer *Hibernia* leaving Holyhead for Dublin on a postcard published in 1905 by her owners, the London & North Western Railway Company, with the large station hotel plainly visible in the background. In 1914 the *Hibernia* was requisitioned by the Admiralty, and in order to avoid confusion with the battleship of the same name, she was re-named *Tara*. Whilst on service in the Mediterranean with the Egyptian Coast Patrol she was torpedoed by an enemy U-boat on 5th November 1915 and sank in eight minutes with the loss of twelve lives.

Trearddur Bay Hotel, before it was extensively altered, shown on a postcard of 1904. Built originally as a family residence by Sir Henry Grayson, a Liverpool shipowner, it was converted into a hotel and run by the Roberts family during the Edwardian years, before being sold to W.H. Williams of Trecastell. But according to Monsarrat, in his description of Trearddur Bay, it was 'unlicensed and indifferently patronized'. Hotels catered mainly for the more affluent visitors where they could live in the style to which they were accustomed, whereas the better-off among the working class generally stayed in boarding houses.

Trearddur Bay Post Office, which was housed in Towyn Stores before being moved to its present location in 1929. By 1911 there had been a thirty-fold increase in the volume of mail handled by the Post Office since the introduction of Uniform Penny Postage in 1840, and Trearddur Bay was one of a number of sub-offices opened in Anglesey during the Edwardian era in order to cope with this huge growth in business. The postcard shows Evan Owen, the sub-postmaster, standing in the shop doorway.

A small group of local residents greet the arrival of the photographer outside the police court at Valley in 1912. The building had been erected eight years earlier and many of the cases heard there during the Edwardian era would today be regarded as trivial. There were prosecutions for riding bicycles without lights, cattle straying, truancy, vagrancy, drunkenness and keeping unlicensed dogs. Poverty-related crimes, such as petty theft, begging and poaching, were also common. Court proceedings were transferred to Holyhead in January 1980, and the building was converted into shop units.

John Jones of Llangefni poses proudly for the camera on his light buggy at the Bodedern Agricultural Show of 1911 after being awarded second prize in the turn-out section for a mare in harness. The eleventh annual show was reported to have been a resounding success, with an attendance of 3,000 and large entries in the various sections for heavy and light horses, cattle, sheep, pigs, dogs, cats, poultry, pigeons, cage birds and horticulture, as well as for pony races and jumping events.

Lower Main Street, Rhosneigr, in 1907. The scene is typical of any Anglesey village on the arrival of a visiting photographer, when children and adults alike would line up and stare curiously at the camera. Rhosneigr had by this time become an attractive seaside holiday resort. It boasted two fashionable hotels, the Bay and the Maelog Lake, where a week's full board cost three guineas, plus a number of 'comfortable furnished apartments'. The opening of the railway station in 1907 helped to popularise the resort even further, and an estimated 2,000 visitors stayed there each week during the summer of 1909.

The old lady, in a flat cap and clogs, seems totally oblivious to the camera as she sweeps the road outside her house in Church Street, Aberffraw, in 1908. The man in the distance, carrying two pails of water from the village pump, is a reminder of what country life was like at the time. The village was almost untouched by outside influences, and largely hidden away from the tourist boom which popularised Anglesey during the Edwardian era. There was a great deal of poverty in Aberffraw, with an average of 129 paupers, or 14 per cent of the population, receiving outdoor relief in 1911.

Bodorgan railway station c. 1905 showing the stationmaster, sporting a straw boater, awaiting the arrival of the train from Holyhead. The board held by one of the porters advertises cheap excursion fares to Bangor. The station was built in 1849 to serve a small scattered community so it was given fewer passenger facilities than most of the other Anglesey main line stations. A goods siding and a coal yard were added in 1851. Bodorgan was one of only three Anglesey intermediary stations to be reprieved by Dr Beeching in 1966.

R.P. Owen. Wheelwright. Bodorgan.

Richard Owen outside his workshop at the station yard, Bodorgan. *Bennett's Business Directory* of 1910 describes him as a 'wheelwright, joiner, timber merchant and coffin maker'. His main trade was in the repair of carts and wagons, but in common with most wheelwrights of the period he also performed a wide range of other tasks, including the manufacture of wheelbarrows, gates, hay rakes and various articles of furniture. Richard Owen was one of only ten wheelwrights enumerated in the Anglesey Census of 1911, and as motor transport replaced the horse-drawn cart their number dwindled rapidly.

Malltraeth Infants School in 1910. The bare-footed little boy seated on the left illustrates the difficulties experienced by parents living below the poverty line. Boots were a constant expense at 3s.11d a pair and clothes had to be bought sparingly, often second-hand, or obtained through charity. Children of the poorest families also suffered from ill-health, bad teeth, defective hearing and impaired vision, which invariably resulted in slow learning.

22580 Llandwyn Island. Life-Boat Launch. Near Carnarvon.

The launch of the *Richard Henry Gould* at Llanddwyn in 1906. This was the first lifeboat station to be established in Anglesey, in 1826. Ten years later the station was closed and the lifeboat transferred to Caernarfon, but it was re-opened by the Anglesey Life-saving Association in 1840. The *Richard Henry Gould* had been sent to Llanddwyn in 1885 to replace the *John Gray Bell*, but during her twenty-two years of service she was only called out ten times. Finally, in 1907, the station was closed as it became increasingly more difficult to recruit a regular crew in such an isolated spot.

A Newborough mat-maker around the turn of the century. The ancient craft of weaving mats out of marram grass, which grew in abundance on the sand dunes, was practised by local women as a cottage industry and sold to farmers as temporary covering for haystacks. Production was later extended to floor mats, strawberry mats, ropes, baskets and fishing nets. Most of the trade was done by barter, which usually worked to the advantage of the buyer, so in order to improve marketing a Mat-makers Association was established in the village during the early 1900s, with a central depot through which the finished products were sold. This gave the industry a sound commercial base from which to expand until competition from machine-made goods finally ended over three centuries of tradition.

Cae Crwn Stores, Newborough c. 1905, with Jane and Robert Williams, the proprietors, standing proudly in the doorway. The shop was also an outlet for locally-made marram mats which were delivered considerable distances by a carrier, who is seen beside his horse. The village constable, known familiarly as 'Wilias Plisman Mawr', keeps a watchful eye on the photographer. Newborough was a thriving place during the Edwardian era. It had a population of 882 and had sufficient local trade to support 11 grocers, 2 of whom had a sideline in drapery, 3 butchers, 2 bootmakers, a baker and a handful of craftsmen.

Caergeiliog, a sleepy village alongside the Holyhead Road, in the days before motor transport plunged the country into a new era. It shows the unhurried way of life of our Edwardian ancestors, with the only traffic being a lady cyclist and a distant cart, on what is today a very busy highway. The Holyhead Road began to be tarred in 1896, at a cost of 2d a yard, to prevent dust in summer and mud in winter, and two years later the county council purchased its first steam roller.

Gwalchmai from East

A peaceful scene on the main Holyhead Road as a farmer delivers milk in the village of Gwalchmai before the First World War. With a population of just 367, Gwalchmai had sufficient local trade in 1910 to support 6 grocers and drapers, 2 butchers, 2 milliners, a baker and confectioner, a bootmaker and a cycle dealer. There were also 3 tea rooms in the village offering 'refreshments for cyclists and commercials'. The cottages on the right have long since been demolished.

The old tollhouse at Gwalchmai, one of five erected on Telford's new road across Anglesey after its completion in 1823. Following a well-established custom, the turnpike gates were let by auction each year, and in 1882 the Gwalchmai gate produced a net income of £45, compared with almost four times that amount before the coming of the railway. The road was freed from tolls in 1895 and its upkeep was transferred from the Turnpike Commissioners to the county council. The tollhouses were sold by auction later that year and the one at Gwalchmai fetched £70, compared with £215 for that at LLanfairpwll.

One of the postcards specially produced by John Roberts in order to advertise his general store at Britannia House, Gaerwen. With fierce competition from 6 grocers and 2 drapers in the village, he had to work hard to survive. Custom was attracted by personal service, the granting of credit and the delivery of goods, all of which were important features of shopkeeping. The reverse side of the card, dated 1912, was used to receipt a customer's order for 3 shirts @ 2s.11d each, 2 vests @ 1/11d, a pinafore for 1s.6d and a pair of stockings for 6d.

A loaded charabanc about to depart from Gaerwen on the annual Sunday School outing c. 1910. This was an exciting adventure, eagerly anticipated by children and adults alike, which enabled them to see something of the wider world beyond the parish pump. At Gaerwen, as in all other Anglesey villages, the lives and activities of most people were centred around the chapel, which had a membership of 384 in 1910. The Sunday School had 254 adherents, 39 per cent of whom were under the age of fifteen, and as many as 40 teachers.

Gaerwen railway station c. 1912. This was built in 1849, the year after the opening of the line from Llanfairpwll to Holyhead. In 1864 it became the junction for the Amlwch branch, which can be seen in the distance leaving the main line. It was, therefore, a busy station, and in 1908 no fewer than 28 trains were stopping there each weekday - 12 locals between Bangor and Holyhead and 16 to or from Amlwch. The station was closed to all traffic in February 1966.

The first passenger train about to depart from Holland Arms station on the opening of the branch line to the temporary terminus at Pentraeth on 1st July 1908. The locomotive used on the service was a Webb 2-4-0 tank (No. 1000), and to avoid having to run this around the train for the return journey a cab was provided for the driver at the rear of the last coach so that he could control the engine from that end.

MENAI HOTEL, Foel Ferry, Brynsiencyn, Anglesey.
Proprietor, H. BERNARD.

Best Situated Hotel in Wales for Scenery, Boating, and Fishing.

The Tal-y-Foel Ferry, which can be traced back to the fifteenth century, linked the Dwyran area with Caernarfon. In 1874 it was purchased by Caernarfon Corporation from the Crown for £458, but it was never widely used and ran at an average loss of £144 a year up to 1914. Business continued to decline until finally, in 1954, Parliamentary approval was obtained to discontinue the service. The small complex of buildings on the Anglesey shore included the Menai Hotel and a wholesale grocery warehouse, run initially by W.I. Jones, and later by the Foel Agricultural Co-operative Society.

The main road looking south east through the village of Llanfairpwll c. 1905, a scene which vanished for ever with the coming of motor transport. A tinker's donkey cart, a familiar sight in Edwardian Anglesey, can be seen near the cottages on the right. These, together with the Wesleyan chapel beyond, are on the site now occupied by the Kwik Save store. The public house at the end of the block of houses on the left is the Butcher's Arms, which offered 'good stabling and carriages for hire'.

The extensive premises of W & O Pritchard, Garneddwen, Llanfairpwll. Conveniently situated opposite the railway station, the brothers William and Owen had built up a thriving business as builders and contractors, undertakers, general merchants, grocers and ironmongers. They also found time to publish postcards of interesting local views. The business was sold in 1922 but the two shops are still in existence today, under new management and with altered frontages.

Passengers crossing the line from the down platform at Llanfairpwll station before the bridge was built. The original station building was a wooden structure, 'ill-fitted for passenger accommodation', and reported to be the worst on the entire stretch of line. In 1865 it caught fire and was rebuilt in stone by John Thomas of Bangor at a cost of £2,200. The station was closed in 1966 under the Beeching axe, but following public pressure it re-opened on 7th May 1973, the first of two Anglesey stations to be reprieved.

Evan Roberts, the evangelist, arriving in LLanfairpwll during his revivalist tour of Anglesey in June 1905, accompanied in the leading group by Rev Charles Williams of Menai Bridge, Professor John Morris Jones and Rev John Williams, Brynsiencyn. His visit was given extensive coverage in the local press, with graphic accounts of the spontaneous frenzy of his converts. But compared with other areas the revival met with little success in Llanfairpwll and Menai Bridge, and by the autumn of 1905 its influence had waned. The postcard was produced by R. Davies of Star Stores, Gaerwen, who was astute enough to see its commercial possibilities.

Llanfairpwll Post Office in 1914, housed in the former Railway Hotel, now re-named Ty Gwyn. This was its second location, having moved there from Tan y Coed the previous year, and it remained there until 1937, the building being leased to the Post Office for £25 a year. The sub-postmistress was Edith Roberts, who held office from 1902 until her death in 1928. She had an establishment of two town postmen, two rural postmen and three telegram boys, who between them delivered an average of 7,863 letters, 247 parcels and 100 telegrams each week of 1914.

The founder members of Llanfairpwll Women's Institute pose proudly for the camera in the garden of 'Y Graig' on 11th September 1915. This was the first Institute to be formed in Great Britain. Six years later a new building near the tollgate was made available and monthly meetings have been held there ever since. Today there are 8,780 Institutes in England and Wales, with a total membership of 301,000.

A decorated arch spanning the Holyhead Road on the outskirts of Llanfairpwll to celebrate the Coronation of Edward VII in August 1902. The Edwardians had a great affection for the new King as he had been a popular Prince of Wales. Tea parties were held throughout the county and children were presented with souvenir mugs. At Beaumaris a dinner was provided for all those over the age of fifty, with each man being given an ounce of tobacco and each woman two ounces of tea. The weather was hot enough for the approaching ladies to have opened their parasoles as a protection against the sun.

A fête at Plas Newydd to celebrate the Investiture of the Prince of Wales at Caernarfon in July 1911, one of several outdoor events held locally. The Edwardians had a strong feeling of patriotism and affection for the Royal Family so tea parties were organised for the children, bonfires lit in the evening, and at nearby Llanfairpwll a floral arch was erected across the road, all providing a welcome relief from the monotony and drudgery of work. The five young ladies seen posing in their finery outside W.R. Jones's marquee were all from Llanfairpwll.

The Marquess of Anglesey at the wheel of his new car, with an elegantly-dressed chauffeur standing alongside. It was a red and cream 16 h.p. Panhard-Levassor, a top-of-the-range French car with a forward-mounted engine, large acetylene lamps and inflated tyres. It was registered in February 1904 as EY 27, but it had a relatively short life at Plas Newydd as the Marquess died the following year at the age of thirty. The car was sold in London in January 1906.

Welsh comic postcards were very popular with English visitors, especially those depicting the name Llanfairpwll............gogogoch. This card was published by the firm of Thomas Bros of Liverpool in its 'Everton' series and was headed 'Llythyr Gerdyn' (Postcard) on the reverse side, with postal and address instructions printed bilingually. Nearly 4,000 different numbered postcards were produced in this series, as well as hundreds of un-numbered ones. Other firms also published Welsh humour cards for the tourist market but none were as prolific as those of Thomas Bros.